Asif Khan

Asif is an award winning writer and actor, born in Bradford. He studied at the University Of Bradford, before training as an actor at RADA. Asif's debut play *Combustion* toured the UK in 2017 and was nominated for OffWestEnd's Best New Play award and Best Writer in the Stage Debut Awards. It also won Best Production at The Eastern Eye Arts, Culture and Theatre Awards (2018) and at The Asian Media Awards (2017). In 2018, Asif won the Channel 4 Playwright's Scheme Award with Rifco and Watford Palace Theatre, where he was commissioned to develop a new play. In 2019, his play *Imaam Imraan* was produced by the National Youth Theatre, playing at the Bradford Literary Festival. He is a Tamasha Theatre Alumnus with whom he has developed two plays for teenagers. Part of the BBC Comedy Room in 2017, he was named on the BBC New Talent Hotlist (2017). In 2015, Asif set up AIK Productions to produce new, high quality theatre, specialising in stories and voices from minority backgrounds. Previous AIK productions include: *Combustion* and *Love Bombs & Apples*. Find out more at: www.theasifkhan.com

First published in the UK in 2022 by Aurora Metro Publications Ltd.

67 Grove Avenue, Twickenham, TW1 4HX

www.aurorametro.com   info@aurorametro.com

FB/AuroraMetroBooks Twitter @aurorametro

Instagram aurora_metro

Jabala and the Jinn copyright © 2022 Asif Khan

Cover image copyright © 2020 Nadine Kaadan

With many thanks to: Saranki Sriranganathan, Abduljabbar Alsuhili, Hassan Adbulrazzak, Saffiya Ingar, Salman Akthar, Jay Varsani, Stratford Circus, The Amal Foundation, Kala Sangam, The Richard Carne Trust, Alaknanda Samarth, Alexandra Cory, Ellen McGahey, The team at Turtle Key Arts, Oli Cambell Smith, Qasim Mahmood, The team at The Belgrade Theatre Coventry, Lyric Hammersmith, Nadine Kadaan, Natalie Davies, Nooh Zia Khan, Charlotte Cunningham, Rosamunde Hutt, Asra Ziaulla

All rights are strictly reserved.

For rights enquiries including performing rights, please contact the publisher: rights@aurorametro.com

No part of this publication may be reproduced, stored in or introduced into a retrieval system, or transmitted in any form, or by any means (electronic, mechanical, photocopying, recording or otherwise) without the prior permission of the publisher. Any person who does any unauthorised act in relation to this publication may be liable to criminal prosecution and civil claims for damages.

This paperback is sold subject to the condition that it shall not, by way of trade or otherwise, be lent, resold, hired out, or otherwise circulated without the publisher's prior consent in any form of binding or cover other than that in which it is published and without a similar condition being imposed on the subsequent purchaser.

Printed in the UK by 4edge printers

ISBNs:

978-1- (print) : 978-1-912430-70-3

978-1- (ebook) 978-1-912430-71-0

Jabala
AND THE
Jinn

by
ASIF KHAN

AURORA METRO BOOKS

Photographs by Mila Sanders

For my little boy, Nooh

CONTENTS

About the Company 6
Biographies 10
Writer's Note 16
JABALA AND THE JINN 17

JABALA AND THE JINN TOUR

**BRADFORD, Kala Sangam, Sat 19 – Sun 20 Feb 11am & 2pm
01274 303 340, kalasangam.org**

**BIRMINGHAM, Midlands Art Centre, Sat 26 – Sun 27 Feb 2pm
0121 446 3232, acbirmingham.co.uk**

**WOLVERHAMPTON, Arena Theatre, Sat 12 March 2pm, Sun 13
March 11am and 2pm, 01902 321 321, arena.wlv.ac.uk**

**LONDON, artsdepot, Sun 20 March 12pm & 3pm,
020 8369 5454. artsdepot.co.uk**

**LONDON, The Studio, Lyric Hammersmith, Sat 2 – Sat 9 April
11am and 1pm, 020 8741 6850, lyric.co.uk**

**POOLE, Lighthouse, Tues 12 April 11am and 2pm,
01202 280000, lighthousepoole.co.uk**

**EXETER, Phoenix, Tues 19 Apr 11am and 2pm, 01392667080
exeterphoenix.org.uk**

**IPSWICH, New Wolsey Theatre, Fri 22 April 2pm,
01473 295900 wolseytheatre.co.uk**

Jabala and the Jinn was made in association with Kala Sangam and the Belgrade Theatre Coventry supported by Stratford Circus and The AMAL Foundation. Funded by Arts Council England.

ABOUT THE COMPANY

Original Cast and Creative Team for filmed and streamed premiere at the Belgrade Theatre, Coventry (2021):

PRODUCERS – Turtle Key Arts/AIK Productions
WRITER – Asif Khan
DIRECTOR – Rosamunde Hutt
ACTOR – Natalie Davies
ACTOR – Safiyya Ingar
ACTOR – Jay Varsani
ORIGINAL MUSIC COMPOSITIONS – James Hesford
SET DESIGN & COSTUME – Mila Sanders
LIGHTING DESIGNER – Aideen Malone
LIGHTING ASSISTANT – Holly Ellis
PRODUCTION MANAGER – Stacey Potter
ILLUSTRATION – Nadine Kaadan

Cast and Creative Team for Live Tour 2022

ACTOR – Natalie Davies
ACTOR – Sara Mazzanti
ACTOR – Riad Richie
ACTOR/UNDERSTUDY – Anshula Bain
TECHNICAL STAGE MANAGER – David Coull
PRODUCTION MANAGER – Stacey Potter

Outreach Workshop Team

Qasim Mahmood
Mez Galaria
Safiyya Ingar
Oliver Campbell-Smith
Natalie Davies

TURTLE KEY ARTS

Turtle Key Arts produces and devises original, inclusive art to entertain and inspire. They believe that access to the arts helps to improve the quality of life by bringing people together, offering creative opportunities, social interaction, confidence and self-esteem.

They produce a number of innovative and original theatre, dance and circus companies and have a long track record of running excellent arts projects, free to all participants, for disabled, disadvantaged and socially excluded people.

Turtle Key Arts unlocks creative potential in individuals, companies and communities, producing and devising original, ground-breaking, inclusive art to entertain and inspire.

As creative producers they enable each project to reach its full artistic potential and ensure that participation and education is embedded at the heart of everything they do.

Their work has a UK and international reach through a wide variety of innovative projects with many different collaborators and partners, currently including the companies: Ockham's Razor, Amici Dance Theatre Company, Open Sky, AIK Productions, Oddly Moving, Kill the Cat and Hassan Abdulrazzak, and recent collaborations with English Touring Opera, Royal College of Music, Lyric Hammersmith, The Wigmore Hall, National Portrait Gallery, The Royal Court Theatre, University of Oxford.

They have played a committed role in advancing participation in the arts by disabled, disadvantaged, and socially excluded people, and are widely recognised as a leader in this field, often charting new territories, such as *Turtle Song* for people with Dementia and *The Key Club* for young people with Autism.

ABOUT THE COMPANY

Turtle Key Arts was formed in 1989 as a unique and ground-breaking accessible space, and accessibility for all continues to be a key philosophy of the company.

TURTLE KEY ARTS

Artistic Director – Charlotte Cunningham
Chief Executive – Alison King
Marketing & Development Director – Shaun Dawson
Senior Producer – Holly Cameron-Jennings
Producer – Kelly Bray
Finance Manager – Alan Bowyer
Project and Office Assistant – Niamh Hanns
Participation Manager – Ruth Naylor-Smith
Dementia Consultant – Carolyn von stumm
Autism Consultant – Ceri Black
Associate Artist for Inclusion – Oliver Campbell Smith

www.turtlekeyarts.org.uk

kalasangam

BIOGRAPHIES

Cast

Natalie Davies – Jabala

Natalie was born and brought up in Bradford of mixed Asian and English parentage. She trained at Northumbria University. Natalie's television credits include *Casualty, Doctors,* and the 2020 Christmas *Vicar of Dibley* shorts (all BBC), and *Coronation Street* (ITV). She will soon be seen playing Ashley in new Channel 4 Comedy *Hullraisers*. She also plays Parveen in the award winning feature film *Eaten By Lions*.

For stage Natalie's credits include her own show *Full English* which recently won Best Production at Asian Media Awards 2021. Other theatre credits include *This Space is Occupied , Northern School* (Bent Architect) and *North Country (*Freedom studios).

Recent BBC Radio 4 credits include *Bangla Bantems* by Kamal Khan and *The War After The War* (Woolyback productions).

Sara Mazzanti – Jinn

With over 25 years performing experience, Sara is absolutely thrilled to be portraying the mysterious and dazzling entity that is the Jinn. Being the playful spirit that she is, and living her life by the phrase 'the creative adult is the child that survived' it is the perfect role for a timeless being who is centuries old.

Sara spent last year working in Berlin on an immersive theatre event set outside the Volksbühne. After the huge success of the first performances she is due to return there after the tour in May. Sara is passionate about art through movement, spiritual enlightenment and the plant based lifestyle.

Born and raised in Leeds, Sara spent much of her childhood visiting family in Bradford which holds a special place in her heart. She is honoured and delighted to encapsulate the Bradford spirit in the form of such a beautiful story.

Riad Richie – Munir/Dad

Riad is of mixed Scottish Moroccan heritage and grew up in East London. He trained at East 15 and has delivered dynamic and engaging performances on stage and screen.

Theatre includes: *The Comedy of Errors* (RSC Tour); *The Whip, A Museum in Baghdad* (RSC); *A Midsummer Night's Dream* (Shakespeare in the Squares); *The Show in which Hopefully Nothing Happens* (Unicorn Theatre); *Tartuffe, Timon of Athens, Tamburlaine* (RSC); Macbeth, *Frankenstein* (Ovalhouse); *Romeo and Juliet* (Theatre Royal Bath); *Mark and the Marked, Getting There, Passenger, Merchant of Venice* (Box Clever); *Saturday Night Fever* (Troxy); *The Scarlet Pimpernel* (Tower of London); *Dick Turpin, LOL, The Changeling* (Clifftown Theatre).

Film Includes: *Romeo & Juliet; Jude Starbeam and the Mind Mission; Asylum.*

Other: Special Action/Combat: Lead Fencer for Disney in Kenneth Branagh's *Cinderella*. Combat for Adam Randalls *iBoy*, Jesse V Johnson's *Accident Man*, Suj Ahmed's *The Gates of Vanity, Future Cinema* with BBC's The Musketeers and Martin Kemp's *Top Dog*.

Anshula Bain – Jabala/Understudy

Anshula first worked with the writer Asif in his National Youth Theatre play *Imaam Imraan* as a young actor. She then made her professional debut in The RSC's *Tartuffe* at The Birmingham Rep. Sadly, the play was postponed due to the pandemic, but she is so excited to step into the role of Jabala on the second half of this incredible tour.

Creatives

Rosamunde Hutt – Director

Rosamunde has led or co-led three major companies, Hijinx Theatre 1990-1993; Theatre Centre, Director, 1993 -2007; Unicorn, Associate Artistic Director, 2007-2011 and is Artistic Director of Pursued by a Bear for whom she directed *Nothing on Earth: Shorts*, 5 digital films by Anna Reynolds (2020) and produced *Pigeons and Plantain* by Afia Nkrumah (Watford Fringe 2021). She has previously collaborated with Asif Khan and Turtle Key Arts on the award winning production of *Love, Bombs and Apples* by Hassan Abdulrazzak (Arcola, UK tour, Golden Thread Productions, San Francisco, and the Kennedy Centre, Washington DC 2019 World Stages season). Recent credits include *New Nigerians* by Oladipo Agboluaje (Arcola and UK tour), *This Evil Thing* by Michael Mears (UK and US tours) and the development of *The Shadow World Musical,* book by Hassan Abdulrazzak, music and lyrics by Karl Lewkowicz. She has worked as a director and producer in India, Romania, Japan and Bangladesh and regularly directs at RADA, Goldsmiths and East 15 School of Acting.

Mila Sanders – Designer

Mila trained at the University of Wales, Aberystwyth and Wimbledon School of Art. Her designs include: *Combustion* (Tara / AIK productions), *Love, Bombs and Apples* (Arcola, UK Tour, San Francisco and The Kennedy Centre), *Imaam Imraan* (National Youth Theatre), *The Pixie and the Pudding* (Little Angel), *The Little Mochi*

Man (A Thousand Cranes), *Soapbox* (Talawa), *Pinocchio, The Wind in the Willows* (Birmingham Old Rep), *The Only Way is Chelsea's* (York Theatre Royal), *Queen of the Nile* (Hull Truck), *Dogs Barking* (RADA), *Parallax, The Door Never Closes, All the Little Things We Crushed* (Almeida).

As costume designer: *A Midsummer Night's Dream, Macbeth, Twelfth Night* (National Theatre), *Jason and the Argonauts* and *St George and the Dragon* (Warwick Arts Centre). Mila is the resident designer at East 15 Acting School and is an associate artist with All Change Arts. www.milasanders.co.uk

James Hesford – Composer

James Hesford is an award-winning musician and composer working in Film, TV and Theatre as well as receiving regular commissions for contemporary orchestral and chamber music. James was born in a mining village in South Yorkshire (UK) and began performing in his early teens in soul and blues bands, touring Europe and the UK. After moving to London, at the age of 19, he studied Fine Art at Sir John Cass and Goldsmiths School of Art. Taking advantage of their music department, he frequently gate crashed lectures on 20th century compositional techniques taking a particular interest in the scores of Stockhausen, Varèse and John Cage. During this period he established himself as a leading jazz guitarist and won the Arts Council's GLAA Young Jazz Musician of the Year Award. The next two years were spent in New York composing and performing all styles of jazz – from bebop to free atonal improvisation – as well as playing in punk bands. Now resident in the UK, James continues to develop his unique compositional style, drawing inspiration as much from his early rock, soul and jazz roots, as from late 20th century contemporary classical music.

Aideen Malone – Lighting Designer

Theatre credits include: *Hamlet* (Young Vic); *Old Bridge* (Bush); *A Kind Of People* (Royal Court); *Death of a Salesman* (Young Vic / Piccadilly); *A Monster Calls* (Old Vic & Bristol Old Vic); *Brighton Rock and A View From A Bridge* (York Theatre Royal); *La Strada* (The Other Palace); *Jane Eyre* and *Peter Pan* (National Theatre & Bristol Old Vic); *Fiddler On The Roof / Conquest To The North Pole* (Liverpool Everyman); *Hetty Feather* (Duke of York); *Frankenstein* (Living Spit); *Napoleon Disrobed* and *The Strange Tale of Stan Laurel and Charlie Chaplin* (Told By An Idiot); *A Raisin in the Sun* and *Talent* (Sheffield Theatre).

Musical credits include: *Carousel* (Regents Park Open Air Theatre); *Talent* (Crucible); *Worst Witch* (Vaudeville).

Dance credits include: *Outwitting The Devil* and *Kaash* (Akram Khan Co); *Darbar Festival* (Sadlers Wells); *Raft* (GED); *Unkindest Cut* (Sadhana); *Time Over Distance Over Time* (Liz Roche); *La Tete* (Jasmin Vardimon).

Opera credits include: *Ariodante, Turn of the Screw, The Marriage of Figaro, A Midsummers Night's Dream, Mary Queen of Scots, Cosi Fan Tutte, Jenufa* and *Tosca* (English Touring Opera).

Future Productions: *Running With Lions* (Lyric); *Wonder Boy* (Bristol Old Vic).

Stacey Potter – Production Manager

Stacey has worked in the arts for over 30 years as a Production Manager, Technical Stage Manager and Company Stage Manager. She has been involved with individuals, companies and festivals producing circus, experimental work and more traditional pieces.

Credits include: *This Time* (Ockham's Razor), *Article 19* (Proud & Loud Arts), *Love Bombs and Apples* & *Jabala*

And The Jinn (AiK Productions), *Oreo,* (Tania Camara), *The Chairs* (Extant), *Flight Paths* (Extant & New Earth Theatre), *Transit, Cinema, Heart* (Zendeh Productions), *Rule 35* (Community Arts Northwest), *Whose Sari Now?* & *Handlooms* (Rasa Productions), *Happily Ever After* (Action Transport), *Manchester Street Poems* (MIF), *Thumbelina* (Dancing Brick), *What Is It?* (PrefaceMorn Dance Theatre), *Lost in the Neuron Forest* (Bread & Goose), *Baby Balloon* & *If All The World Were Paper* (Oily Cart).

David Coull – Technical Stage Manager

David graduated from the University of Derby in July 2020 with a first-class honors degree in

Technical Theatre. Working as a Theatre technician, with an emphasis on Lighting Design and Production LX. Working across the UK in theatres including Derby Theatre & The Lighthouse Theatre, Kettering. Recently establishing his own business, Carpe Noctem, offering Lighting, Sound & amp, Stage solutions to the UK. This is David's debut tour and he is delighted to be working with such a brilliant company on an amazing performance. Previous productions include: *Barnum* (Derby Theatre, 2018); *Blood Brothers* (Derby Theatre, 2019); *Peter Pan* (Lighthouse Theatre, 2020). Lighting design work includes: *The Pillowman* (2019, Derby Theatre); *Seven Acts of Mercy* (2020, Derby Theatre); *Derby Rises* (2020, Derby Theatre); *Northern Girls* (2021, Pilot Theatre); *Sleeping Beauty* (2021, Duchess Theatre)

About the Play

I have a little boy, who is five. As a parent, you often worry about the challenges our children may face – challenges which we ourselves faced when we were kids. One of those challenges, which I only fully understood as an adult, was the effects of never seeing myself represented. Growing up noticing that all the 'cool' people on television, in sport, in music, in films, in stories, in plays, never included anyone who looked like me. This led me to believe that being 'brown' was not cool, and being a 'Muslim' was not cool either. I felt a little embarrassed and ashamed about my background and desperately wanted to fit in. This is something I never want my little boy to feel. And so because there is a lack of stories for children involving British Muslim characters, I thought 'why not write some myself ?!'

Kala Sangam, Stratford Circus and The Amal Foundation sent out an invite for a new piece of children's theatre, involving British Muslim themes. I pitched the idea for *Jabala and the Jinn* and we were offered some money to explore it further with actors and a director. The inspiring few days of conversations and improvising, led to me walking away feeling I had the whole story worked out in my head.

Unfortunately, just as we were preparing for a tour of the play, we were hit by the Covid-19 pandemic forcing theatres to close. Our only option was to do a live-streamed performance of the play and the Belgrade Theatre (Coventry) were instrumental in providing us with this fantastic opportunity.

Now in 2022, we have been given another opportunity to tour and I am incredibly excited to finally see this play performed to live audiences.

JABALA AND THE JINN

The first live stage production was at Kala Sangam, Bradford, on 19th February, 2022, directed by Rosamunde Hutt.

Characters

JABALA
MUNIR
DAD
JINN (SARAH)

Notes:
A forward slash (/) in the dialogue = an interruption
Beat = short pause
Pause = slightly longer
Silence = even longer!

SCENE 1

Jabala's house.

DAD *(Voice off stage)* Jabala! Hurry up!

Jabala runs onto centre stage and speaks directly to the audience.

JABALA Hi! I'm Jabala. Full name Jabala Khan.

DAD Jabala!

JABALA That's ma dad. Getting a bit angry coz we're late for school. Again.

DAD Come down and get your coat and shoes on!

JABALA I'm the champion at being late for school. But it's sooo hard getting out of ma comfy bed in the morning. Why does staying in bed always feel better in the morning? At night time I hate going to bed!

DAD Don't make me come upstairs!

JABALA So dad's always a bit grumpy in the morning. But at all other times he's really nice. He normally calls me 'sweetie' or 'my baby' or 'Jabsi'.

DAD Jabala!

JABALA But when he's grumpy he calls me 'Jabala'. I'd love to keep chatting but I better go before

Dad's voice starts getting squeaky. That's what happens when he's really grumpy.

DAD *(high pitched)* Jabala!

JABALA Ooops, too late!

Dad rushes on with Jabala's coat and shoes.

DAD Quick, quick, quick, quick, quick...

Jabala, now hurrying, puts on her coat and shoes. Dad runs out, off stage, to the car outside with her school bag. Jabala goes to follow.

Then stops.

JABALA *(To the house)* Assalaamu-alaycum.

(To audience) My mum always used to do that when she left the house.

DAD *(even higher pitch)* Jabala!

JABALA See ya!

Jabala runs off.

SCENE 2

School playground. Noise of kids playing in the background.

JABALA In the playground the girls normally play footy on the grass there. And the boys play games in this area. Right over there is Amy. She's the prettiest girl. And the cleverest. And the best at sports. She's pretty much the bestest at everything really. And she's got loads of friends. I tried to be her friend a few times, but she said 'no'. Hopefully one day though. That's my dream.

Munir appears. He speaks broken English in an Arabic accent.

MUNIR	Hello!
JABALA	Goodbye!
MUNIR	You play game... me.
JABALA	I told you I don't wanna play your stupid game.
MUNIR	You say word... English. I put in head. Brain.
JABALA	No!
MUNIR	Say word. English.
JABALA	No! Do you know that word? 'No'?!

MUNIR	You know 'Shakispeah'?
JABALA	You what?
MUNIR	Shakispeah! He famous. English famous!
JABALA	You mean 'Shakespeare'?
MUNIR	Yes! Shakispeah! You know?
JABALA	Yeah... he wrote stories like a gazillion years ago.
MUNIR	Yes! Like Romeo Juliet! I like. I Romeo. You Juliet.
JABALA	Aren't they like girlfriend and boyfriend?
MUNIR	Yes!
JABALA	No chance!
MUNIR	Me want be... Shakispeah... learn Shakispeah... be Romeo. Then I be famous. Like home. In home I is famous.
JABALA	Famous?
MUNIR	Yes! Famous! You know... TV. I actor in TV. Famous!
JABALA	Yeah right!
MUNIR	True! Arabic TV. Arabic drama. Then war. What you say? *(He makes the sound of guns)*
JABALA	Hosepipe?
MUNIR	No. Not this.

He continues making the sound of guns.

JABALA	Guns?
MUNIR	Yes, guns! And... *(makes the sound of a bomb exploding)*

JABALA Water balloon?

MUNIR Not this.

He continues making the sound of a bomb.

JABALA Bomb?

MUNIR Yes, bomb! Big bomb. Many bomb. People die. Father die.

JABALA Oh.

MUNIR So I come here. England. My mum bring England.

JABALA Where did you come from?

MUNIR I come Yemen.

JABALA Is that near Scotland?

MUNIR Many miles. Very bad. So I come England. Then speak English. Speak the Shakispeah. Then Famous. Money. House. No school. No need school. You understand?

JABALA If you're wanting to bunk off school you've got no chance.

School bell rings.

JABALA *(To audience)* Did he say his daddy died? If so, maybe I should be a bit nicer to him? Even though he's so annoying! My mummy died... so I know it's not nice. It's made me quite sad. Very sad, actually. But Daddy said to not be too sad, coz she's gone to heaven and we'll see her again.

SCENE 3

Jabala's home. Kitchen.

JABALA The next morning...

DAD *(Voice off stage)* Jabala! Hurry up!

JABALA We were late. Again. Told you it always happens.

Dad rushes on with Jabala's coat and shoes.

DAD Quick, quick, quick, quick, quick...

Jabala now hurrying, puts on her coat and shoes. Dad runs out to the car with her school bag. Jabala goes to follow. Then stops.

JABALA *(To the house)* Assalaamu-alaycum.

JINN *(A voice off stage)* Wa-alaycum-assalaam.

Jabala stops. Turns back. Pause.

JABALA *(To the house)* Hello?

No response.

JABALA *(To audience)* Was it just me or did you hear that too? *(To the house)* Hello?

No response.

JABALA *(To the house)* Goodbye?

No response.

JABALA Mummy?

No response.

JABALA *(To the house)* Assalaamu-alaycum.

JINN Wa-alaycum-assalaam.

JABALA *(Stunned)* Huh?! Who is that?!

No response.

JABALA *(To the house)* Assalaamu-alaycum.

JINN Wa-alaycum-assalaam.

JABALA Inshallah.

JINN Inshallah.

DAD *(From outside, high pitched)* Jabala!

JABALA Coming Daddy!

She runs out.

SCENE 4

Playground.

MUNIR So now want be friend?

JABALA Yes.

MUNIR Why this? Before you say 'No!'... 'go away!'... thing like this.

JABALA	Look, do you want to be friends or what?!
MUNIR	You English teach?
JABALA	Yes!
MUNIR	Shakispeah?
JABALA	Yes! But nobody can see that we're friends.
MUNIR	Why this?
JABALA	Amy finally agreed to be my friend yesterday. For a trial period. But only if I stay away from 'refugee boy'.
MUNIR	Who 'refugee boy'?
JABALA	You!
MUNIR	Oh.
JABALA	And also she said I've gotta change my name to summat else... something more English. So whatever you do... do not call me Jabala if she's around. I'm 'Ruth' alright?
MUNIR	Ruth?
JABALA	Yeah. Ruth.
MUNIR	OK. Friend. Ruth. We play word English game?
JABALA	No.
MUNIR	You not good friend Ruth.
JABALA	What language do you speak?
MUNIR	I English speak!

JABALA No I mean before you came to England. Do you speak the same language as the word 'assalaamu-alaycum'.

MUNIR Yes. 'Peace be upon you'. Arabic.

JABALA You definitely speak Arabic?

MUNIR Yes. I speakish Arabic.

JABALA Right. *(Jabala notices Amy close by)* Quick! Separate!

MUNIR Why?

JABALA Amy, you dummy!

MUNIR Oh.

Jabala and Munir move to separate sides of the stage, so as not to be seen together and continue the rest of the dialogue like this.

JABALA Now stay there. Don't come closer!

MUNIR OK. I stay here Jabala.

JABALA Ruth!

MUNIR Ruth!

JABALA Now...

Jabala continues to watch anxiously where Amy is in the playground.

MUNIR Yes?

JABALA How would you like to come over to my house after school for orange juice?

MUNIR Me come your house?

JABALA Yes, my house. I'll have to ask my daddy first obviously. So will you come?

MUNIR	Yes! Yes! I come. I come Jabala house!
JABALA	Ruth!
MUNIR	Ruth house!

SCENE 5

Kitchen table at Jabala's house. They're both drinking orange juice and eating peanut butter toasties.

MUNIR	Orange juice very nice, Ruth!
JABALA	You don't have to call me Ruth now. Only at school.
MUNIR	Orange juice very nice Jabala!
JABALA	Yeah ma daddy squeezes it fresh for me everyday.
MUNIR	Daddy very nice!
JABALA	And he makes the best peanut butter toasties.
MUNIR	So...

Munir pulls out a tiny copy of 'Romeo and Juliet'.

MUNIR	Ready teach Shakispeah?
JABALA	Not yet. First I need to tell you summat.
MUNIR	Tell?
JABALA	Yes, coz I need your help.
MUNIR	Munir help Ruth problem no.

JABALA No need to call me Ruth I said.

MUNIR Problem no.

JABALA You see. Now don't get spooked out or nothing. But yesterday when I left the house I heard summat.

MUNIR No understand.

JABALA Like a voice. I said sommat and then the voice said summat back. And I think... I think... it might be my mummy.

MUNIR Mummy?

JABALA Yeah, my mummy. Coz she died like a few months ago.

MUNIR Oh. I sorry.

JABALA Yeah.

MUNIR Not nice this.

JABALA Yeah. But you know... I think she might still be around... as like a ghost.

Beat.

MUNIR This joke?

JABALA No, it's not.

MUNIR This joke! Very funny comedy joke.

JABALA Honestly, I'm not joking, Munir!

MUNIR So ghost... Mummy ghost... here?

JABALA Yes!

MUNIR Well bring! Bring ghost!

JABALA Thing is... for some reason... I think the ghost... Mummy can't speak English.

MUNIR	Well how speak?
JABALA	Well, I think it speaks in Arabic?
MUNIR	Jabala Mummy Arabic?
JABALA	No.
MUNIR	Well how can be Mummy if Arabic speak?
JABALA	I don't know!
MUNIR	Well, I Arabic speak.
JABALA	Yes, that's why I invited you over! You think I actually wanted to be your friend?!
MUNIR	Oh.
JABALA	So can you say summat in Arabic now to it?
MUNIR	Say what? Where?
JABALA	Just say summat like... 'What's your name?'
MUNIR	Say this to you?
JABALA	No! Up there somewhere.
MUNIR	Up there?
JABALA	Yes! Wait.
MUNIR	What?
JABALA	Let me just check on Daddy.

Jabala goes to look out of the window.

JABALA	Still gardening. Right. Go on then.
MUNIR	Up here?
JABALA	Yeah.

MUNIR	OK. *(In Arabic)* What's your name?

No response.

MUNIR	See! No hear nothing.
JABALA	Say it again. Say 'Assalaamu-laycum' first.
MUNIR	Assalaamu-alaycum.
JINN	Wa-alaycum-assalaam.

Both Jabala and Munir gasp. Munir is now terrified and hides behind a chair.

JABALA	See! Did you hear that?!
MUNIR	Yes. Yes. I hear.
JABALA	Told you!
MUNIR	This your father?
JABALA	My daddy doesn't speak like a girl. Ask it its name?
MUNIR	No, I no ask.
JABALA	What?
MUNIR	This not good. This very bad.
JABALA	Why?
MUNIR	This jinn!
JABALA	Jinn?
MUNIR	Yes, you know... Jinn!
JABALA	What's that?
MUNIR	You don't know jinn? All Muslim peoples know jinns.

JABALA	I don't.
MUNIR	Well I tell you. Jinn. This jinn. I leave.

Munir turns to go.

JABALA	No!
MUNIR	Yes, I go. Thank you orange juice.
JABALA	Stop! You're not going anywhere!
MUNIR	I no like this!
JABALA	Ask it its name?
MUNIR	No!
JABALA	Munir please... I'll teach you every English word I know!

Beat.

MUNIR	Every word?
JABALA	Yes!
MUNIR	How many every?
JABALA	Like... five thousand!
MUNIR	This many word?
JABALA	Deal?

Pause.

MUNIR	One time. Then go.
JABALA	OK!

MUNIR *(Arabic)* What's your name?

JINN *(Arabic)* My name is Sarah.

JABALA	What she say? Did she say her name was 'Sarah'?

MUNIR   Yes. 'Sarah'.

JABALA   But my mummy's name is 'Kausar'.

MUNIR   This not your mummy! This jinn! Scary jinn!

JABALA   Relax! Ask it something else. Ask it who it is... what it is?

MUNIR *(Arabic)* Who are you?

JINN *(Arabic)* I told you, I'm Sarah! If you want to know more then grab some garlic, stick it under a cup and place one finger on the cup.

JABALA   What did it say?

MUNIR   It said...

JABALA   Yes?

Beat.

MUNIR   You have garlic?

JABALA   Garlic?!

MUNIR   It ask me. Get garlic. Do this.

JABALA   Right.

Jabala looks in a kitchen bowl and pulls out some garlic.

JABALA   Here.

MUNIR   Now cup. Clean cup.

JABALA   Cup?

MUNIR   It ask me!

JABALA   OK.

Jabala gets a cup. Gives it to Munir. Munir places the

garlic under cup.

JABALA What you doing?

MUNIR Put finger here.

JABALA Why?

Munir's facial expression gives her the answer.

JABALA Sorry. Yes. Understood. 'It ask you'.

Munir puts his finger on the cup with the garlic underneath.

MUNIR Like this.

JABALA This is weird!

Jabala does as told.

MUNIR (*To Jinn in Arabic*) We've done what you said. Now what?

JINN (*Arabic*) Now say... three times... 'Magic garlic, magic garlic, do your magic.'

MUNIR OK. (*To Jabala*) This say. (*Arabic*) 'Magic garlic, magic garlic, do your magic.'

JABALA You what?

MUNIR It say speak this.

JABALA Right.

MUNIR Ready?

JABALA What does it mean?

MUNIR It mean... 'Magic garlic, magic garlic, do your magic.'

JABALA Oh...

MUNIR Ready or no?

JABALA Ready!

MUNIR *(Arabic)* 'Magic garlic, magic garlic, do your magic.'

JABALA *(Arabic)* 'Magic garlic, magic garlic, do your magic.'

MUNIR Again. *(Arabic)* 'Magic garlic, magic garlic, do your magic.'

JABALA *(Arabic)* 'Magic garlic, magic garlic, do your magic.'

MUNIR Last time. *(Arabic)* 'Magic garlic, magic garlic, do your magic.'

JABALA *(Arabic)* 'Magic garlic, magic garlic, do your magic.'

There's silence for a good few seconds. Munir and Jabala are confused.

JABALA What? What's supposed to happen?

Then on walks Sarah, the Jinn, unseen.

A girl of the same age and in every way like an ordinary girl. She speaks English in a Bradford accent.

JABALA Is that garlic supposed to disappear or summat?

Sarah walks up to the kitchen table and drinks Munir's glass of orange juice. Jabala and Munir watch, completely bewildered.

JINN You weren't lying! This orange juice is well wicked man!

JABALA Who are you?!

JINN	Sarah.
MUNIR	What?
JINN	Sarah. Pleased to meet you! Handshake!

No response.

JINN No! Fist bump? I've seen you humans do this a lot. Gimme some skin!

She puts out her fist. Tentatively, Jabala reponds.

JINN Man. I always wondered what it would be like to have skin. It's wicked! *(To Munir)* Now you. Handshake! No, fist bump! Gimme some skin!

Munir is nervous about responding.

JINN	Gimme some skin man!
MUNIR	What you?
JINN	Sarah!
MUNIR	No. What you? How you?
JINN	Oh. Yeah, I'm a jinn.

Beat.

JINN Well, not right now, coz you guys just made me human, which is sick! But normally, yeah, I'm a jinn. I live in this house as well.

JABALA This house?

JINN Yeah! I live here with you guys... but I don't live here with you guys... there's a space... a space yeah... it's here but it's not here... OK right... so you see I done this... Yah! *(she karate chops her hand through the air)*... see that... that air... I kind of live in that.

JABALA I'm confused.

JINN It's just like your house, 'cept this is ma mum and dad's room... and your bathroom is our kitchen and my room... it's within the cracks in your attic.

MUNIR *(Terrified)* Jabala?

JABALA Yes?

MUNIR I scream?

JABALA Don't you dare. Ma dad's just outside.

MUNIR Small scream?

JABALA No! *(To Jinn)* So like... how long have you like... lived here?

JINN In this house? Since you were born. In Bradford? Seven centuries.

JABALA Seven centuries?!

JINN Yeah.

JABALA Isn't like... a century supposed to be one hundred years?

MUNIR Yes.

JINN Yeah... you know like your seven years old?

JABALA Yeah.

JINN Well, I'm seven years old as well... 'cept in your human years it's seven hundred years... quite simple... you get me?

JABALA No.

JINN Doesn't matter.

JABALA So are you like a ghost?

MUNIR Yes!

JINN Not a ghost.

MUNIR Yes! Jinn, ghost! I know jinn! I know jinn story!

JINN Don't tell me you believe all that made up 'Aladdin' stuff? All that 'rubbing the magic lamp' nonsense?!

JABALA To be honest, I didn't even know what a jinn was.

JINN Well, I'm just like you. I like playing games, toys, messing around, doing naughty things. All o'that!

JABALA Right.

JINN But the jinn world is boring, man. I'm an only child and jinns don't go to school, so I got no one to play with, you get me?

JABALA Right.

JINN So I wondered if you wanna pal up?

JABALA Pal up?

JINN Be friends, innit? Play games?

JABALA What game?

JINN 'Skyball'?

JABALA 'Skyball'?

JINN Wait... no... you guys can't fly.

JABALA You can fly?!

JINN How about 'Teleport and Seek'?

JABALA 'Teleport and Seek'?

JINN Wait! You guys can't teleport.

JABALA   What's teleport?

JINN   When you go invisible and re-appear somewhere else.

JABALA   You can go invisible?!

JINN   Yeah.

JABALA   That's amazing.

JINN   Is it?

JABALA   Yeah!

JINN   It's pretty boring to me.

JABALA   No it's not!

JINN   Trust me... after seven centuries... teleporting gets dull.

JABALA   Can you teach us?

JINN   Nah, sorry. There's certain jinn stuff I can't teach humans.

JABALA   Oh, that's not fair.

JINN   Listen. There's certain stuff you got that I don't... and if I could swap... I would.

JABALA   Would ya?

JINN   Yeah! You guys have so much fun... and you have this skin... and arms and legs. And you play wicked games like 'Grandma's Footsteps' and... what's that game where you run around after each other?

MUNIR   Tag?

JINN   Yeah tag! Let's play tag.

She quickly tags Munir.

JINN   You're it!

Jinn runs off. Then Jabala runs off. After a few seconds Munir reluctantly joins in the game. He can't catch them. There's laughter and noise.

JABALA Wait. *(Goes to window)* Yes, Daddy?... OK, Daddy! *(To Munir and Jinn)* We've gotta keep the noise down.

Jinn tags Munir.

JINN Tag! You're it!

MUNIR Why me, always!

We suddenly hear a weird bleeping noise.

JABALA What's that?

JINN My alarm. So unfair! Ma time's nearly up... I gotta go.

JABALA Why?!

JINN But I really liked being your friend.

JABALA Us too!

JINN So you promise you'll bring me back? Make me human again?

JABALA Yeah, always!

JINN Wicked! Let's play tag in the playground! Tomorrow! At your school! I'll follow you in!

JABALA That'll be ace!

JINN Don't forget the magic words!

JABALA 'Magic garlic, magic garlic, do your magic.'

JINN In Arabic!

We hear the weird bleeping noise intensify, sucking Sarah back into the jinn world.

JABALA   I can't remember it now!

JINN   He can! And don't forget the garlic!

Jinn disappears.

JINN   And the cup!

Silence.

Munir and Jabala look at each other in disbelief. Gobsmacked.

JABALA   That was...

MUNIR   What?

JABALA   Jinn-tastic.

SCENE 6

Early hours of the morning. Dad is up rummaging through various suitcases, drawers etc, looking for something, getting more and more frustrated. After a few seconds, Jabala enters.

JABALA   Daddy?

DAD   Sweetie. Go back to bed, please.

JABALA   What are you doing? It's really messy in here!

DAD Jabsi, you didn't take Mummy's bracelet from my drawer, did you?

JABALA No.

DAD The one with the little diamond in it?

JABALA Yeah the one we both gave her for Mother's Day?

DAD Yeah, you didn't take it, did you?

JABALA No.

DAD Look I won't be angry, just tell me the truth. Did you take it?

JABALA No, I didn't.

DAD Right.

Dad goes back to searching.

JABALA Daddy, do you want me to help?

DAD No, it's OK, sweetie, go back to sleep. You gotta wake up for school soon.

JABALA I'll help you.

DAD No Jabala.

JABALA I'll help.

DAD *(Shouts)* I said go back to bed!

Beat.

JABALA Daddy, why are you angry?

DAD I'm not angry I'm...

Dad slowly makes his way to the floor, head in hands. He's clearly extremely upset.

JABALA Daddy, why are you sad?

Pause.

JABALA You said not to be sad, remember?

DAD I'm not sad, sweetie, I'm not...

JABALA Yes you are. You've got tears in your eyes and everything.

DAD I'm fine, my baby, don't worry.

JABALA I've never seen you cry before. I don't like it.

DAD Come here.

They hug.

JABALA Are you sad because of the bracelet?

DAD Yes... it was very special... to me... because it was Mummy's.

JABALA We'll find it. I'll find it.

DAD I'm sure we will.

JABALA I promise, I'll find it.

DAD Yeah. Listen sweetie, let's get you back to bed. I'll read you another chapter of Matilda, yeah?

JABALA Two chapters?

DAD Yeah. Two chapters.

A beat. They smile at each other.

JABALA *(To audience)* I made him read me five.

SCENE 7

Playground.

MUNIR   Ruth!

JABALA   It's OK, you can call me Jabala now.

MUNIR   Why, Ruth?

JABALA   Coz she's already seen me playing with you, thats why!

MUNIR   Oh.

JABALA   And her mummy told her not to play with us two.

MUNIR   Why this?

JABALA   Don't know. Listen. You didn't see a gold bracelet at my house yesterday, did you?

MUNIR   Gold brace? No.

JABALA   Never mind.

MUNIR   Why?

JABALA   My dad lost it. It used to be ma mum's and he was crying last night.

MUNIR   Oh. This sad.

JABALA   Yeah.

Beat.

MUNIR	Why not find?
JABALA	You think I haven't already tried?!
MUNIR	Oh.
JABALA	Yeah.
MUNIR	Why not give gift?
JABALA	Gift?
MUNIR	Yes. Gift. Make happy. Father happy.
JABALA	Like what?
MUNIR	Err... make food. Make special dinner... juice... special sandwich... thing like this?
JABALA	It is Eid soon.
MUNIR	Yes! Eid gift!
JABALA	First one without Mummy. He's definitely gonna get upset.
MUNIR	Then do Eid special sandwich! Make special Eid dinner. Father like this.
JABALA	OK. Yeah. OK, I will do.

Beat.

JABALA	Thanks.
MUNIR	Problem no.
JABALA	No problem.
MUNIR	No problem. And I got thing make you happy.
JABALA	What?

Munir pulls out some garlic and a small cup. Jabala smiles.

They go through the ritual of bringing Sarah into the human world again.

MUNIR/JABALA *(Arabic)* 'Magic garlic, magic garlic, do your magic. Magic garlic, magic garlic, do your magic. Magic garlic, magic garlic, do your magic.

Sarah appears.

JINN Handshake! No fist bump! No hug!

JABALA Sarah!

Jabala goes straight in for the hug.

JINN *(To Munir)* You! Handshake! No fist pump! No hug!

Munir is still a bit nervous about making physical contact.

JINN Oh I get it. Still scared of the jinn.

JABALA He's not scared. Are you Munir?

MUNIR No. Not scared.

JABALA So, hug?

MUNIR Yes.

He tentatively goes ahead to hug. As soon as he makes contact with Sarah, she screams, which frightens the life out of Munir.

MUNIR Aaahhhh!

Sarah and Jabala laugh.

JINN Your face!

MUNIR Not funny.

JABALA Hilarious!

MUNIR	This not funny.
JABALA	OK, let's play a game.
MUNIR	No. Not play now.
JABALA	Oh come on, Munir.
MUNIR	You not nice.
JINN	How about we play any game you like?
JABALA	Yeah, you choose?
JINN	Your choice!
MUNIR	Any choice?
JABALA	Yeah, your choice.
MUNIR	I choose...
JABALA	What?
MUNIR	Shakispeah!

He pulls out his copy of Romeo and Juliet.

JABALA	Not Shakespeare! That's not even a game!
MUNIR	Yes, game! You teach Shakispeah.
JABALA	Nooo!
MUNIR	Remember, you say you teach.
JABALA	Sarah doesn't wanna play Shakespeare!
JINN	Hang on. I don't mind Shakespeare.
JABALA	Really?
JINN	Yeah, I know that one really good. 'Romeo and Juliet'. Know all the words to it and everything.

MUNIR You know this?

JINN Yeah! I've met Shakespeare.

MUNIR Met Shakispeah?!

JINN Yeah... centuries ago... when he was living. Well, when I say met... I mean... I kinda played some naughty jokes on him.

JABALA What like?

JINN You know. Took his quill and hid it places. Swapped some pages from *King Lear* to *Twelfth Night*. Ha, ha! Come on test me... say any line!

Munir flicks through and finds a Romeo line.

MUNIR 'But soft/

JINN What light through yonder window breaks... it is the east, and Juliet is the sun'.

Munir amazed, picks another line from elsewhere in the text.

MUNIR 'See how she leans her cheek upon/

JINN 'her hand! O that I were a glove upon that hand, That I might touch that cheek!'

MUNIR Wow! You teach Shakispeah!

JABALA The most boring game ever!

SCENE 8

JABALA *(To audience)* So the *(like Munir)* 'Shakispeah' game took up all of Sarah's time. Then the weird sound happened again...

(Weird bleeping noise as before.)

...and Sarah had to go back to jinn world. Coz she could only stay human for a few minutes at a time.

(Bleeping stops.)

But then we brought her back after school! Then at playtime again! And after school again! Every chance we got, we brought Sarah back! All week! And we were having so much fun! I didn't even care about nasty Amy anymore, whether she wanted to be my friend or not. Coz now I had Sarah!

Music. A rap, sung by Jinn. Jabala and Munir join in for the chorus and maybe accompany in other ways too e.g. beatbox, live instrument. Or a recorded track can be used. A dance sequence should be included too and fancy lighting.

ALL

Magic garlic, magic garlic do your magic
Magic garlic, magic garlic do your magic
Magic garlic, magic garlic do your magic
I'm a Jinn
I'm a Jinn
I'm a Jinn so I don't have skin
Having human flesh is my thing

But I'm living in a separate world
'Invisibility' is the word
Similar to yours
Doing Mum's chores
Early bedtime
Shortening ma playtime
Grumpy Dad
Gettin grounded when I'm bad
Mm mm
No fun makes me mad
Mm mm
No friends makes me sad
How'ma gonna play?
Alone in ma alleyway
A boring existence
Despite my persistence
Mm mm
I need some assistance
Mm mm
I'm needing some assistants
A human friendship
To play in ma spaceship
Games till we're delirious
Fantastical experience
Freeze tag
Tunnel tag
Elbow tag
Turtle tag
I'm a playful character

With max fun register
A fierce competitor
I'm quicker and slicker
Mm mm
In any games you might deliver
Mm mm
But it wasn't gonna happen
Ma fantasy was shaken
Ma dreams were all broken
So I found a way
So I don't have to stay
A magical sequence
A secret password
The answer to ma dreams
And it goes like
It goes like
It goes like
Magic garlic, magic garlic do your magic
Magic garlic, magic garlic do your magic
Magic garlic, magic garlic do your magic

The sequence signifies a passage of time over one week. Jabala, Sarah and Munir make mess everywhere in the fun.

It's then interrupted by Dad walking across, in a different imaginary space to the rest, slowly tidying up the mess.

JABALA But I was still worried about my daddy. We still couldn't find Mummy's bracelet and even though he put on a smile and took me to karate practice, I could tell by his eyes he was sad. Coz when you're sad... your eyes look sad... and his eyes were sad. Munir and Sarah started helping me plan Daddy's surprise and I couldn't wait for it to be Eid now. I didn't care that I was getting a present myself. I just wanted to make my daddy's eyes smile.

SCENE 9

Jabala's back garden.

JINN Handshake! No fist pump! No hug! No fusion!

MUNIR Fusion!

They shape their arms into a big C, connect via fingers and act out an electric bolt of energy.

JINN/MUNIR Zzz!

JINN Where's Jabala?

MUNIR Inside house. Find skipping rope.

JINN Yes, man!

Munir has spotted a bracelet round Sarah's wrist.

MUNIR What this?

JINN What's what?

MUNIR This. Thing. On arm.

JINN *(Realising)* Nothing.

She hides her arm behind her back.

JINN	Forgot to take it off.
MUNIR	Me show.
JINN	No.
MUNIR	Let see this.
JINN	I said no.
MUNIR	This Jabala bracelet?
JINN	No!

MUNIR   Then show. Why no show? If nothing bad, then me show.

Sarah reluctantly puts her arm out to show Munir the bracelet.

MUNIR	Oh, Sarah.
JINN	What?
MUNIR	This bad. This very bad.
JINN	Why?
MUNIR	This same Jabala Mother bracelet.
JINN	No it isn't!

MUNIR   Same as she say. Gold. Diamond. Even say Jabala name… Look. 'Happy Mother's Day, Love from Jabala and Daddy.'

Beat.

MUNIR   You steal this?

Beat.

JINN	You gonna tell Jabala?
MUNIR	No.
JINN	Phew.
MUNIR	You tell Jabala.
JINN	I can't do that!
MUNIR	Yes! Can!
JINN	Please!
MUNIR	Jabala very sad. Jabala daddy very sad.
JINN	I know!
MUNIR	Then give this Jabala. Say sorry.
JINN	No!
MUNIR	Well, you not good friend.
JINN	I am a good friend!
MUNIR	You nasty evil jinn.
JINN	I did it for Jabala, alright!
MUNIR	What?
JINN	I did it to be her friend forever. Just don't tell her, please.

She takes it off and puts it in her pocket.

MUNIR   If you no tell Jabala, me tell Jabala.

Jabala runs into the garden to join them with her skipping rope.

JABALA   Found it!

JINN   Yeah! Handshake! No fist pump! No hug! No fusion!

JABALA   Fusion!

JINN/JABALA Zzz!

JABALA   Right altogether!

JINN/JABALA Fusion!

Munir doesn't join in the ritual.

JABALA   Come on Munir! Fusion!

Munir still doesn't respond. Sarah is looking nervous.

MUNIR *(To Jinn)* I say? Or you say?

JABALA   Say what?

MUNIR   She not good friend, Jabala.

JABALA   What? What you talking about?

MUNIR   Your mother bracelet – she steal.

Pause.

JABALA   Is that true, Sarah?

JINN   Look, I stole it before we made proper friends alright!

JABALA   You've had my mummy's bracelet this whole time?!

JINN   I kept it safe alright. In ma jinn bedroom.

JABALA   You know how upset my daddy is because of that bracelet.

JINN   I know but/

JABALA   Then why did you steal it?

JINN   I did it to be your friend!

JABALA   You were my friend!

JINN To be your friend forever alright! I don't wanna be a jinn anymore, I wanna be human!

JABALA What d'you mean?

JINN I need this bracelet.

JABALA Why?

JINN Coz it's gold! And it's got a diamond too!

JABALA And?

JINN That's two of the seven things I need!

JABALA What?

JINN Some gold, a diamond, ten grams of human hair, a tablespoon of garden soil, a mug of water, three slugs and fifteen acorns. I've gotta get these things.

JABALA Why?

JINN So I can melt it all down, mix it together and drink it!

JABALA/MUNIR You what?!

JINN Ma grandma told me.

MUNIR This congusting!

JABALA 'Disgusting', Munir.

MUNIR Disgusting!

JINN If I get those seven different things and make it into a jinn smoothie and drink it, then I can change into a human being forever. Forever! Not for a few minutes, before I'm pulled back into jinn world. I can stay here, with you, be human, be your friend, forever! Us three, best friends, forever! Playing games and having fun, forever!

Beat.

JABALA   I don't know what to say.

JINN   You can say, I can keep the bracelet? Your dad... well... he's moved on now... he's lost it... he'll be fine... he's probably forgotten about it already. I only need ten grams of your hair now and then I'm human!

Jinn reaches for Jabala's hair.

JABALA   No!

JINN   You don't wanna be my friend?

JABALA   I did. But my dad... he's the most special thing to me. And he's heartbroken because of that bracelet. And you... you... what's that word?

JINN   'Betrayed'?

JABALA   Yeah. You betrayed me.

MUNIR   Good word. 'Betrayed'.

Beat.

JABALA   I'd like my mummy's bracelet back please.

Beat.

JINN   No.

MUNIR   Just give, Sarah.

JINN   Shut up you, ya grasser! You can't even speak English properly! I taught you Shakespeare... I was gonna teach you all the other Shakespeares... and that's how you repay me?!

JABALA *(stern)* Give me my mummy's bracelet back. Now.

JINN I can be really nasty you know... I'm much stronger than you both... put together... I can use all my powers and do lots of nasty things... so you two better watch out!

We hear the weird beeping noise calling Sarah back to the jinn world.

JINN Yeah, I get it now. You humans stick together! I should have listened to my auntie... she said you humans can't be trusted. Forget about me, the jinn, the non-human! Just coz I don't have skin. All I ever wanted was to be like you and be your friend forever, but it looks like you two don't care, so you can take your stupid bracelet back!

She takes it out and throws it back to Jabala.

JINN There!

Jabala picks it up.

JABALA This is the last time you'll ever be in our world, coz I will never, ever, say those magic garlic words again.

Jinn disappears.

SCENE 10

Jabala's kitchen.

JABALA Biscuits?
MUNIR Check.

JABALA	Cheese and onion crisps?
MUNIR	Check.
JABALA	OK that's the starters ticked off.
JABALA	Jam sandwiches?
MUNIR	Check.
JABALA	Peanut butter sandwiches?
MUNIR	Check.
JABALA	Cheese spread sandwiches?
MUNIR	Check.
JABALA	OK, that's main course. Fizzy Cola bottles?
MUNIR	Check.
JABALA	Jelly babies?
MUNIR	Check.
JABALA	OK, that's dessert. Looks like we're done!
MUNIR	Yes.
JABALA	What's the time?
MUNIR	Exactly 9.54am.
JABALA	OK. I told Dad to come down at 10 o'clock.
MUNIR	10 o'clock?!
JABALA	Yes, why?
MUNIR	But my performance practice?!
JABALA	You did it fine yesterday.
MUNIR	But one time practice here!

JABALA	OK. Quick. Ready?
MUNIR	Yes.

They get to their rehearsed positions.

JABALA And for your special Eid surprise, we have my best friend Munir, performing Romeo. Let the performance begin!

Munir walks on, super intense and stands on the chair opposite where Dad will sit. He directs his monologue directly into where Dad's eyes will be.

MUNIR But soft! What light through yonder window breaks?

   It is the East, and Juliet is the sun!

   Arise, fair sun, and kill the envious moon,

   Who is already sick and pale with grief

   That thou her maid art far more fair than she.

   Be not her maid, since she is envious.

   Her vestal livery is but sick and green,

   And none but fools do wear it. Cast it off.

   It is my lady; O, it is my love!

   O that she knew she were/

Sound of Dad in the background.

JABALA Oh no! Dad! He's coming, quick hide!

Munir exits to hide outside. Jabala makes some last minute preparations, dusts Dad's chair, tidies the table and then puts on Dad's favourite music — Stevie Wonder.

Dad enters.

JABALA Eid Mubarak, Daddy!

DAD Eid Mubarak, baby! What's this?

JABALA It's a special Eid dinner surprise breakfast!

DAD For me?

JABALA Yeah! So if you'd like to take a seat here, please, sir.

She pulls out a chair for Dad.

DAD *(Playing along)* Oh, thank you.

She tucks a napkin into his shirt.

DAD Nice music.

JABALA I borrowed it from your collection.

DAD My favourite.

JABALA I know. Stevie Wonderful.

DAD 'Wonder,' darling.

JABALA 'Wonder'. I hope you're hungry, coz I've prepared a full three course meal.

DAD I'm starving!

JABALA For starters we have biscuits and cheese and onions crisps!

DAD Mmm.

She serves Dad and sits next to him.

DAD This is very kind of you, sweetie.

JABALA My pleasure! And also... I was gonna save it till the end but...

She pulls out her mum's bracelet. Beat.

DAD	Where did you find it?!
JABALA	It was in your orange boots!

Dad stares at it, tears in eyes, clearly very emotional. He hugs Jabala. A moment.

DAD	I love you.
JABALA	I love you too, Daddy.

Pause.

JABALA Now I hope you like Shakespeare?

DAD Why?

JABALA *(Shouts)* Let the performance begin!!

SCENE 11

Dad rushes on with Jabala's coat and shoes.

DAD Quick, quick, quick, quick, quick...

Jabala now hurrying, puts on her coat and shoes. Dad runs out to the car outside with her school bag. Jabala goes to follow.

Then stops. Thinks for a moment.

She quickly grabs some garlic from the bowl and places it under a cup.

JABALA *(To audience)* What d'you think? Shall I?

Beat.

JABALA *(Arabic)* 'Magic garlic, magic garlic, do your magic.' 'Magic garlic, magic garlic, do your magic.' 'Magic garlic, magic garlic, do your magic.'

In comes Jinn.

JINN I thought you weren't going to bring me back?

JABALA Yeah... well...

Beat.

JINN I'm sorry, OK. Really sorry.

JABALA It's OK.

JINN I'm a terrible jinn.

JABALA Very terrible.

JINN I know I did a bad thing, but it's only coz I really really wanted to be human.

JABALA I know.

JINN But it's probably a better choice to stay a jinn coz I'd miss ma mum and dad.

JABALA I understand.

JINN Did you have a good Eid?

JABALA Yeah. Dad loved the Eid dinner and Munir smashed it.

JINN I know. I was watching.

Beat.

JINN I'm glad your dad is happy again.

DAD *(From outside)* Jabala!

JABALA Not right now, he isn't. I'd better go.

JINN OK. I'll see ya then.

Beat.

JABALA I'm gonna take this garlic and cup with me. See you at playtime?

The jinn smiles.

JINN See you at playtime.

JABALA Assalaamu-alaycum.

JINN Wa-alaycum-assalaam.

DAD *(high pitched)* Jabala!

JABALA Coming!!

Jabala runs off.

Lights down.

The End.

Also available by Asif Khan from
www.aurorametro.com

Combustion
£9.99
ISBN 9781911501923

You may also like:

Homing Birds by Rukhsana Ahmad
£9.99
ISBN 9781912430451